THE STORY OF TWENTY-FIVE YEARS

HIS MAJESTY KING GEORGE V.

News Chronicle

STORY OF
TWENTY-FIVE
YEARS

Compiled by

W. J. MAKIN

*Celebrating the Royal
Silver Jubilee, 1910–1935*

With over 300 half-tone Illustrations

London

GEORGE NEWNES LIMITED

Southampton Street, Strand, W.C. 2

PRINTED IN GREAT BRITAIN BY
BILLING AND SONS LTD., GUILDFORD AND ESHER

ACKNOWLEDGMENT

THE compiler of this record of *The Story of Twenty-Five Years* wishes to express his indebtedness to many anonymous journalists for descriptive matter appearing in the newspaper files of the period. Also to the authors and publishers of the following books:

War Diaries. By Lord Riddell. (Ivor Nicholson and Watson.)

Intimate Diary of the Peace Conference and After. By Lord Riddell. (Gollancz.)

A Modern History of the English People. By R. H. Gretton. (Martin Secker.)

Ourselves 1900-1930. By Irene Clephane. (The Bodley Head.)

How We Lived Then. By Mrs. C. S. Peel, O.B.E. (The Bodley Head.)

King George V. By Sir George Arthur. (Jonathan Cape.)

England's Royal Family. By Colonel R. J. Blackham. (Sampson Low.)

These Hurrying Years. By Gerald Heard. (Chatto and Windus.)

King Edward VII. and His Times. By André Maurois. (Cassell.)

First War in the Air. By R. H. Kiernan. (Peter Davies.)

Celebrated Spies. By George Barton. (Page.)

A Brief History of Our Times. By Ramsay Muir. (Philip.)

The Encyclopædia Britannica.

By Air. By Sir Harry Brittain. (Hutchinson.)

The A B C of the B.B.C. By Sir Harry Brittain. (Pearson.)

Finally, the thanks of the compiler are due also to Mr. Ewart Williams for his help in the selection of the photographs and the reading of the manuscript.

WILLIAM J. MAKIN.

18, HENRIETTA STREET,
LONDON, W.C. 2.

CONTENTS

LIST OF ILLUSTRATIONS

CHAPTER I

BIRTH OF A NEW AGE

Illness of King Edward VII.—His death—Proclaiming the new King—King George's youth—"The Sailor Prince"—His marriage to Princess May—Training him for the Throne.

I

A GREY-BEARDED man sat at a tea-table in a room in Buckingham Palace. He looked tired and ill. From his chair he could see the bright green of lawn and trees shaded by the sunshine of a May afternoon.

Fumbling for a cigar, he put it between his lips and lit it with an air of finality. But he had only taken a few puffs when he was seized with a paroxysm of coughing. Large brown patches appeared on the familiar face. His hands trembled.

The door opened quietly. A frock-coated medical man approached the coughing figure.

"Your Majesty!" he begged. "These cigars . . ."

Britain's greatest diplomat, King Edward VII., gazed with tear-dimmed eyes, brought on by the coughing, at his medical attendant and tried to wave him away. But the medical man had glimpsed something else. By the tea-table was a mass of official documents that the King had been perusing.

"Your Majesty," he again pleaded, "I implore you to rest."

With an effort, King Edward recovered his breath.

"No, no," he wheezed, shaking his head. "I shall work to the end. . . . Of what use is it to be alive if one cannot work?"

The medical man shrugged his shoulders. A gesture from the King and he withdrew. But no sooner had the door closed than the grey-bearded man, clutching the cigar between his fingers, was once again doubled by a fit of coughing.

This time it was a good four minutes before he recovered. He breathed noisily and painfully.

"If this lasts much longer," he muttered to himself, "I am done for."

An hour later he was receiving a high colonial official and discussing with an effort matters of State. As the official left Buckingham Palace, he was heard to remark: "I have seen a dying man."

Meanwhile, in another room of the Palace, other medical men had gathered. A Cabinet Minister. Also the King's Private Secretary. It was still the tradition in Britain that the illness of royalty should, unless terribly serious, be kept secret from the public. At the same time it was decided to send an urgent telegram to Queen Alexandra, who was at Corfu.

"It is best that the Queen return at once," decided the doctors.

Hurriedly, the Private Secretary composed a telegram, and, by means of official channels, it was flashed towards that island in the Mediterranean.

On the morning of May 6, 1910, the doctors examined King Edward. He was very ill. The heart was failing. Yet the King was ominously calm. He refused to stay in bed. He dressed himself fully, and sat again in that room overlooking the Palace gardens. At one period he walked painfully to the other side of the Palace and looked down towards the Mall. A criss-cross of scaffolding and grey tarpaulin covered the huge mass that was to be a monument to Queen Victoria, a work in progress.

"I shall never live to see it unveiled," he nodded, a strange smile hiding itself beneath the beard as he thought of that great mother Queen who had chided him as Prince of Wales for his glittering, rather feverish, life.

What was it they had said of him? The dying man struggled to recall the whispers of those about him.

" . . . He likes the society of women who can talk, of Jews and people who can amuse him. And he really likes any public ceremony, and theatres and cards. . . . But he is a sensible man, and knows more about foreign affairs than anyone, and has quite advanced ideas. . . ."

King Edward chuckled. Yes, he had lived his period. Edwardian, they would call it. And many would look back upon it with regret. Few realised at the time that in that dying King was England at her zenith, her richest and most powerful. Even then the clouds were gathering on the horizon. And he, Edward, shrewdest of all the diplomats, had glimpsed them. His many journeys to the Continent had been in the nature of a preparation for the storm.

With a sigh, King Edward wandered back to his sitting-room. He tried to smoke one more cigar, but got no pleasure from it.

"I feel miserably ill," he confessed, laying the cigar aside.

At eleven o'clock he wanted to rise to receive his old friend, Sir Ernest Cassel, who found him in his sitting-room, dressed as usual. The King rose from his arm-chair to shake Cassel's hand, but looked as if he had suffered, and could not speak distinctly. But he still had his kindly smile.

"I am very ill," he murmured, "but I wanted to see you. . . ."

Once again in that other room the medical men had met. This time a public bulletin had to be issued. At the same time the Archbishop of Canterbury was summoned. Rumours began to be whispered through the streets of London. The King was dying; the King was dead. . . .

In the official residence of the Prime Minister, 10, Downing Street, Mrs. Asquith was handing a telegram to a servant. It was addressed to her husband, urging him to return at once. Even as the servant padded away, Lord Kitchener was announced. He entered the room.

"Have you heard the dreadful rumour?" whispered Mrs. Asquith.

Lord Kitchener jerked his head impatiently.

"Absurd!" he snapped. "You've only to look out of the window. The flag on the Palace isn't at half-mast yet."

And indeed the Royal Standard was still flying in the windy May sunshine.

The serious bulletin published at eleven o'clock cast a gloom over the luncheon tables of the West End. At Kempton Park a huge crowd of race-goers anxiously watched the board go up for the 4.15 race. The King's horse, Witch, was scheduled to run. Would it be scratched at the last moment? But a cheer was raised when it was seen that the horse would run after all. And even greater and prolonged cheering greeted the finish of the race with Witch an easy winner. It was considered a happy omen.

Inside Buckingham Palace, the Prince of Wales received the glad news and hurried into the sitting-room to congratulate his father.

The grey-bearded figure nodded, and tried to smile.

"Yes, they told me. . . . I am glad."

A few moments later he slipped into a coma. Queen Alexandra, who had returned from Corfu, herself helped to carry him to his bedroom. He was undressed and laid on the bed.

"I will go on. . . . I will go on. . . ." he muttered determinedly.

But they were the last coherent words King Edward spoke. Even while he was still struggling against death a Privy Council had been summoned to proclaim his successor. And in accordance with tradition a regiment of Life Guards stood by, booted and spurred, ready for emergencies.

Groups of people began to drift towards the Palace. They clustered the railings and stared silently at those lighted windows where a king was fighting his last desperate battle. Some shivered in the cool night air. A woman wrapped a shawl round her baby. Dumb faces stared upwards.

At a quarter to twelve King Edward breathed his last. A member of the Royal Household came down and stepped across the gravel to the railings. His feet crunched nearer and nearer, a messenger of ill-tidings.

He faced the crowd through the railings.

"The King is dead," he said quietly.

A deep silence fell on the crowd. Men fumbled for their hats and removed them. A woman's sob seemed to shake them. The news, though not unexpected, was stunning.

"The King is dead."

That quiet announcement was already flaring and resounding throughout the world. Mr. Asquith, the Prime Minister, at the moment aboard the Admiralty yacht *Enchantress*, pitching full-steam ahead from the Mediterranean to England, received the news at three o'clock in the morning. He rose from his bunk and went on deck.

Above the pitching mast in the pale glow of the dawn, Halley's comet blazed across the sky.

"The King is dead; long live the King!"

King George V. had begun his reign.

II

At half past four the following afternoon, one hundred and fifty Privy Councillors met in the large hall at St. James's Palace. A silent, hushed assembly. No greetings, no handshakes.

Lord Crewe rose from his seat. A strange, tense silence held all who were present.

"The King is dead," announced Lord Crewe simply, "and it is our duty to proclaim his successor."

The Lord Chancellor and the Archbishop of Canterbury then went out of the room. In a few moments they returned. Walking between them was the Prince of Wales, whom Lord Crewe presented to the Council as King George V. After a few words the King took his seat on the throne and all those present knelt before him on a cushion,

2

swearing their loyalty, each in the manner of his faith.

That same evening Mrs. Asquith dined with Winston Churchill and Lord and Lady Crewe. After dinner Churchill rose, and, holding his glass on high, said: "Let us drink to the health of the new King." And Lord Crewe replied: "Or, rather, to the memory of the old."

The black velvet darkness of night was over England. In the Throne Room at Buckingham Palace, four Grenadier Guardsmen, their heads bowed over their reversed rifles, stood at the corners of the coffin in a long, silent vigil. . . .

At nine o'clock on the morning of May 9, 1910, an ancient and picturesque ceremonial was unrolled. A Guard of Honour of the First Life Guards clattered into Friary Court of the Palace, followed by the band of the Coldstream Guards with draped guns. Behind them rode the Army Headquarters staff in full-dress uniform. The red and blue garbed figures stood out against the grey stone background of the Palace.

A great crowd had assembled for the ceremony. A fanfare of trumpets drew all eyes to the balcony overlooking the quadrangle. The State trumpeters had raised their shining instruments. Figures in colourful robes and uniforms stalked on to the balcony. The group included the Duke of Norfolk, Earl Marshal, and Garter King-of-Arms and Pursuivants of the Heralds' College.

From a window of Marlborough House, opposite the quadrangle, three young boys and a girl watched this picturesque ceremonial. They were the children of King George. At another window, though unseen by the people, were the King and Queen.

After that preliminary fanfare of trumpets, there was silence for a few moments. Then the Garter King-of-Arms stepped forward, unrolled a scroll, and began to read in a loud, clear voice.

" . . . Whereas it has pleased Almighty God to call to His Mercy our late Sovereign Lord King Edward the Seventh, of blessed and Glorious Memory, by whose Decease the Imperial Crown of the United Kingdom of Great Britain and Ireland is solely and rightfully come to the High and Mighty Prince George Frederick Ernest Albert:

"We, therefore, the Lords Spiritual and Temporal of this Realm being here assisted with those of His late Majesty's Privy Council, with numbers of other principal gentlemen of quality, with the Lord Mayor, Aldermen and citizens of London, do now hereby, with one voice and content of tongue and heart, publish and proclaim:

"That the High and Mighty Prince George Frederick Ernest Albert is now, by the death of our late Sovereign of happy memory, become our only lawful right Liege Lord George the Fifth by the Grace of God King of the United Kingdom of Great Britain and Ireland, and of the British Dominions beyond the Seas, Defender of the Faith, Emperor of India, to whom we do acknowledge all faith and constant obedience, with all hearty and humble affection, beseeching God, by whom Kings and Queens do reign, to bless the Royal Prince George the Fifth with long and happy years to reign over us. . . ."

As the clear voice of the reader of the proclamation rang out, the troops stood at the salute and the men in the large crowd bared their heads. When the voice of the Garter King-of-Arms ceased there was a breathless silence. Then the Earl Marshal raised his gloved hand.

"God save the King!" he cried.

THE FUNERAL OF KING EDWARD VII. *in May, 1910, saw the death also of an era. The years that followed, with his son as King, were to create a new England.*

EIGHT KINGS *attended the funeral of King Edward VII. At the head of the procession walked the new King and his eldest son, the sixteen-year-old Prince of Wales.*

"God save the King!" cried the crowd in unison, and the roaring sound of the National Anthem echoed from the grey stone walls surrounding the quadrangle.

Even as the crowd sang, the guns began to boom. A Royal Salute of forty-one guns was being fired from the bright green lawns of St. James's Park.

III

"Good old Teddie!" is how a crowd often boisterously received King Edward. If the new King was not spontaneously greeted as "Good old Georgie!" there was, nevertheless, an unqualified note of warm affection and absolute confidence which revealed the respect with which he stood in the eyes of the nation.

Throughout the year that preceded his coronation, King George was discussed, studied and written about with that democratic freedom which is the envy and amazement of Continental nations. The British public wished to know about their new King. And from this searching limelight of publicity there emerged a man, human, and, above all, likeable, who, throughout the years of trial and fortitude that were to follow, never lost the deep affection and loyalty of the nation.

King George was not so jovial as was his father, but he had more urbanity. He was approachable, friendly, and sympathetic in bearing. King Edward would sternly dismiss anyone whom he thought was presuming too far. King George would not hurt the feelings of even the most aggressive by a look of displeasure or annoyance.

Throughout his exacting Royal cavalcade King George has graciously received everyone who approached him, however ordinary. He has bent himself to listen with an air of earnest expectation, as if there was an important message about to be delivered, and when he has heard it he responds with a kindly comment and understanding smile. He has displayed certain simple and fundamental qualities of character which have not only endeared him to the people, but also achieved a more profound devotion than that accorded to his father.

It was at Marlborough House, in June, 1865, that the baby Prince George was born. That there is good, healthy blood in the family has been proved by the remarkable longevity of the present ruling house of England. No ruling member of it has lived for less than 67 years.

George I. was 67 when he died, George II. was 77, George III. 82, George IV. 68, William IV. 72, Queen Victoria 81, and King Edward 69. Our present King, George V., is 69, and, as was manifested on many occasions, it is hoped that he will be spared for several more years.

Although the blood of King George is mainly German, it can safely be said that no more English King ever sat on the throne. Despite the origin of the Coburg family, in its small principality on the fringe of the Thuringian Forest, that branch which came to England soon shed their German trappings. King Edward was essentially an Englishman, and both by early training and environment the young Prince George soon revealed himself as more English than the English. Today, King George is regarded as the very apotheosis of the English gentleman.

Actually the limelight of publicity fell more upon Prince George's elder brother, the Duke of Clarence, who was until his death in 1892 the intended heir to the Throne. Nevertheless, the training of the two young princes proceeded together and was of that rigorous character which prevailed in the Victorian age.

There are engaging incidents on record to give us a picture of Prince George as a boy. Mr. Hector Bolitho, in his new book, *Victoria, the Widow and Her Son,* gives us a glimpse of the 'sixties and 'seventies when the two young princes were growing boys.

Prince George was brought up in awe of his father, whose genial nature never lessened his sense of princely right. But the authority which Edward exercised over his sons was never relentless nor unsympathetic. The healthy spirits of boyhood were never treated brutally at Marlborough House. When Prince George and his elder brother were sent to the training ship *Britannia* they showed " as much healthy naughtiness " as their contemporaries.

There is one enchanting story of a day when the Prince was taken with his brother to Westminster Abbey. Dean Stanley had been asked to show them the treasures of the Abbey. Nobody could make the memorials of Westminster come to life again as Dean Stanley could, with his vivid historic sense. In spite of the charm of the Dean's stories, Prince George wandered away by himself. At last he was found in a dim little side chapel. He had scrambled on top of Queen Elizabeth's tomb, and, looking down at the effigy, he was saying, " What an ugly old woman! "

Prince George was twelve when he became the youngest cadet on board the *Britannia.* He was conscientious; the flame of duty, which was to be an inspiration of his reign, was already alive in him and was an inheritance from his Coburg grandfather. When he was a boy, there were already signs of the similarity in character. The signs were to increase as the years passed. But, in leisure, he was spirited and impish. On one occasion, a couple of marline-spikes found their way into the bed of an officer. A certain cadet was suspected. Then Prince George admitted that he was the culprit and he faced his punishment. His leave was stopped for one week.

Nevertheless, the record of Prince George was that of an efficient officer. He was devotedly attached to his calling, although, like Nelson and other distinguished sailors, he suffered from seasickness. No distinction was made between Prince George and his shipmates. It has been recorded that he was an excellent singer of comic songs and often regaled his shipmates with the latest.

Moreover, he early displayed that keen sense of humour which has remained with him until the present day. Once when his ship was in Turkish waters, a Pasha came on board to pay his respects to the grandson of the Queen of England, and son of the Prince of Wales. It happened that the Prince that day was having his turn in the duty of coaling, and when he appeared on deck from the stokehold, his overalls black and his face and hands grimy with coaldust, even the Oriental calm of the Pasha was ruffled at the sight.

It was when he was serving in H.M.S. *Excellent* that the future King met a certain " Jackie " Fisher, who was then Captain of the Gunnery School. Even in those days the future First Lord of

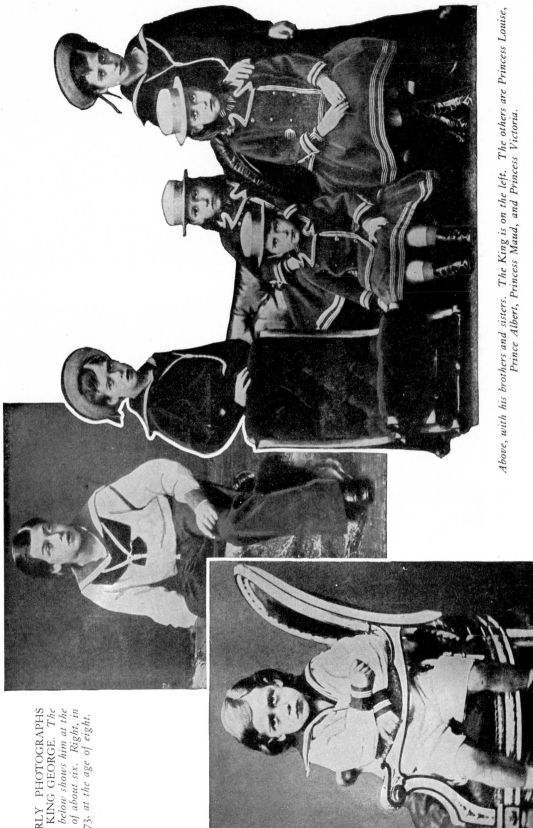

EARLY PHOTOGRAPHS OF KING GEORGE. *The one below shows him at the age of about six. Right, in 1873, at the age of eight.*

Above, with his brothers and sisters. The King is on the left. The others are Princess Louise, Prince Albert, Princess Maud, and Princess Victoria.

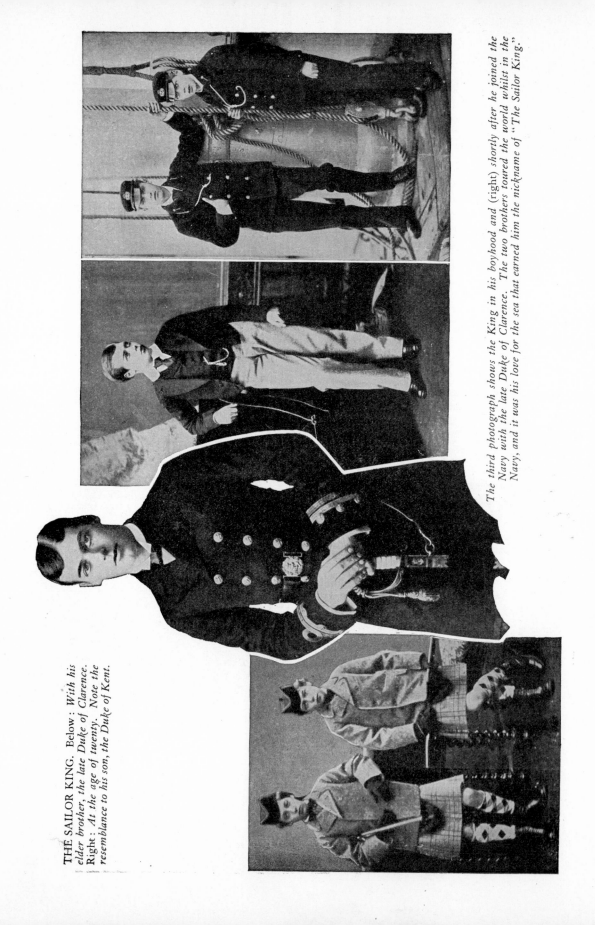

THE SAILOR KING. Below: With his elder brother, the late Duke of Clarence. Right: At the age of twenty. Note the resemblance to his son, the Duke of Kent.

The third photograph shows the King in his boyhood and (right) shortly after he joined the Navy with the late Duke of Clarence. The two brothers toured the world whilst in the Navy, and it was his love for the sea that earned him the nickname of "The Sailor King."

the Admiralty had a perverse temper and an eloquent flow of language, but Prince George appears to have recognised the real and outstanding ability of the man, and formed a real attachment that lasted until the death of Lord Fisher.

Eventually, the two young princes were transferred to the *Bacchante*, in which they toured the world. There was no hint yet that Prince George would become heir to the Throne, through his elder brother's death. He was, therefore, educated as a second son, with the consequent differences in aims and responsibilities. A sailor's life suited him; he was a man's man, and his character and tastes were of the mould that thrives in a wardroom or an officers' mess.

In the *Bacchante* the princes travelled as far as Australia and New Zealand. In Australia they descended a gold mine; they aimed with boomerangs and even ate minced kangaroo. In New Zealand they shook hands with dusky Maori chieftains who had fought against their grandmother's soldiers.

Prince George was at home on both land and sea. He wrote in his Journal: "After dinner much amusement, trying to sit on an empty corked bottle, on the deck, at the same time holding a candle in each hand, one of which was lighted, the other to be lighted from it, without rolling over."

While he was in Australian waters Prince George left the *Bacchante* to stay with an Australian hostess. She made a charming gesture which showed him that graciousness was to flourish as well as corn and wool in the new countries of his grandmother's empire. When he went down for breakfast he found a wreath of rosebuds about his plate.

They were, he was told, "For Sunday morning and in memory of England."

It was during this voyage that the world was startled by a statement widely published in the newspapers that the princes, landing at Bermuda, had each had his nose tattooed with an anchor. It was feared in the Royal Household that the story might be true, because of Prince George's addiction to pranks and practical jokes, for which he was known in the home circle as the "Royal Pickle." Once at a family luncheon at Windsor Castle, in his childhood, he incurred the displeasure of the severe, as well as august, Queen Victoria, and as a punishment was sent under the table until he was in a fit mind to behave himself. After a while he was heard to say, "Grandmamma, I'm quite good now." "Very well, then," said Grandmamma, "you may come out." Out he came, wholly naked and unashamed, having in his banishment divested himself of every bit of clothing. There was no knowing what a boy like that might be up to. Anxious telegrams were sent to the ship, and greatly to the relief of the country, as well as of the Royal Family, it was announced that the story was unfounded. What had happened was that the boys ornamented each other's noses with pollen from the brilliant orange stamens of the Bermuda lilies. From that day to this yellow noses are regarded as the height of fashion in the island, especially by the native ladies.

It was also while a midshipman that Prince George began his hobby of stamp collecting, which today is still one of his chief relaxations. It can be said that the present King George possesses one of the most comprehensive and valuable collections of stamps in the world. It was an excellent hobby for a boy to have chosen. Postage stamps do give a breadth of vision, with the vivid colouring, the heads of potentates, the pictures, and names of far-off places suggestive of romance. As the King once told the Junior Philatelic Society, it was a hobby he had pursued with "unabated interest" throughout the years.

Before he left home for this world voyage he promised his mother to read the Bible daily. The Pocket Testament League in 1912 wrote to Buckingham Palace asking if it was true that King George followed the practice of daily Bible reading. "It is quite true," Lord Knollys, the King's Private Secretary, replied, "that he promised Queen Alexandra as long ago as 1881 that he would read a chapter of the Bible daily, and that he has ever since adhered to this promise."

Always the watchful eye of Queen Victoria was on the young princes. When the *Bacchante* in which her grandsons were serving as midshipmen had been ordered to South Africa, Queen Victoria wrote to her daughter-in-law, Alexandra:

Darling Alix,
I am sorry Bertie (the future King Edward) *should have been sore about the boys; but I think he must have forgotten the arrangements and conditions and instructions respecting their going to sea.*

I, and even Bertie and you, only consented to their both going to sea for their education and moral training. This being the case—the Bacchante *going to the Cape, which was done in a hurry without one consultation with me (I disapproved)—and feeling how valuable these two young lives are to the whole nation, I felt bound to protect them against useless and unnecessary exposure in a cruel Civil War—for so it is, the Boers being my subjects, and it being a rule that Princes of the Royal Family ought not to be mixed in it.*

In any other war, should in time there be one (when Georgie be older), and his ship be obliged to take part in it, I would quite agree with Bertie.

Pray show this to him, as I am sure he and everyone would agree in this being the right course.

But even Queen Victoria could not control the adventures which the young princes encountered on this world tour.

The ship nearly drowned Prince George in the Pacific upon one occasion. They even survived the adventure with a mad nigger of Simonstown who almost killed them in a "spider" drawn by four beautiful white horses, which the Governor had sent over to drive them to Cape Town.

Mad with drink, we are told, the Malay drove headlong up hill and down dale, into the surf of the sea and out of it, crashed into a Cape waggon, and finished upon the spoke of one wheel at Government House, a jubilant man who was at least an optimist.

And in this same region, when sailing round the Cape of Good Hope, our future King and some of those who sailed with him in the *Bacchante* fell in with a phantom ship, and clearly observed that her spars and her sails shone with a fire as of gold.

At the end of the cruise, in 1882, the two brothers parted company. Prince Albert Victor was destined for the Army and the succession to the Throne; Prince George adopted the sea as his avocation. His Englishry was already marked. Truly he could say:

I travelled among unknown men,
In lands beyond the sea;
Nor, England, did I know till then
What love I bore to thee.

Prince George was given his first independent command—Torpedo Boat No. 79. This ship took part in the naval manœuvres of 1889 in some of the worst weather which has ever been experienced on our coasts.

Admiral Penrose Fitzgerald has brought to light an incident in these manœuvres which shows that the King was not only a capable but a very plucky sailor. Three torpedo boats, of which No. 79 was one, had a rendezvous with a senior officer in Lough Swilly. Prince George's little craft turned up in time, but had to report the grave news that one of its companions had engine trouble and had been obliged to cast anchor close to the Donegal coast. The commander of No. 79 reported that he had tried to tow the crippled torpedo boat, but his towing gear had broken. There was nothing to be done except to leave her with the third torpedo boat standing by and report at the rendezvous for fresh hawsers.

The senior naval officer wanted to go to the rescue himself, but with some misgivings gave way to the request of the plucky young commander of No. 79 to let him have another try. A less conscientious commander might well have rested satisfied after spending the previous night trying to assist his companion ship, and leave to a less tired crew than his own the task of dealing with the situation. The future King was, however, made of sterner stuff, so, equipped with a new hawser, he put to sea again in the teeth of a heavy gale.

The work of rescuing the disabled torpedo boat was a job requiring not only courage and initiative, but skilful seamanship, and one of those proud moments which the King must love to recall is when he towed the helpless ship to safety. The incident reveals that the King was in his true element when at sea, and there is reality behind the proud title " Sailor King."

For this achievement Prince George received the post of commander of the first-class gunboat *Thrush*, and later commander of the new second-class cruiser *Melampus*. This commission was designed to be the first of a series of important commands. There was no doubt of the keenness of Prince George. His ambition was that one day he would have the pride and joy of hoisting his Flag as an Admiral on the active list. He used to say how glad he was that he would not have to be King, as he wanted to remain a sailor.

Fate, however, decreed that this command of the *Melampus* was to be his last naval appointment as Prince George. In November, 1891, he was attacked by serious illness, which very nearly brought to an end his career.

The Prince was on a visit to the Curragh, where his brother was quartered with his regiment, the 11th Hussars. He returned to a small family party at Sandringham, but showed signs of being seriously ill. He developed fever and King Edward hurried him off to London, where the doctors diagnosed enteric fever. It was a long struggle, but Prince George came through. His vigorous and healthy constitution resisted the disease germs. But the young Prince had only entered upon the convalescent stage when another tragic event occurred in the English Royal

Family, which was to entirely change the outlook of Prince George.

In January, 1892, by the premature death of his brother Prince Albert Victor, Duke of Clarence, he came into the direct line of succession to the Throne. After sixteen years' continuous service afloat, his career at sea was abruptly terminated. He was raised to the peerage as Duke of York, and was introduced in the House of Lords by his father.

A new and greater career was opening for him.

IV

And so we come to the woman, the first lady of the land, who has played an important and great part in this drama of twenty-five years.

Her Majesty Queen Mary is undoubtedly the most gracious, the most dignified, and most important Queen reigning in the world today. She has endeared herself to the people of this country in no uncertain fashion. She is admired and esteemed, and there is no member of any royal household who takes the duties of royalty so seriously, or who works harder at what is perhaps the most exacting job in the world.

Queen Mary may be said to be a real Londoner. She was born on the stroke of midnight, May 26, 1867, in Kensington Palace, in a room which had been the nursery of Queen Victoria. She is descended from Adolphus, Duke of Cambridge, the seventh son of George III., who married the Princess Augusta, the daughter of the Landgrave of Hesse. The Queen's mother, the Princess Marie Adelaide, was the second daughter of the Duke of Cambridge, and therefore the cousin and a contemporary of

Queen Victoria, but some fourteen years her junior.

At her baptism by the Archbishop of Canterbury, she was given a garland of names—Victoria Mary Augusta Louisa Olga Pauline Claudine Agnes—only to have them all reduced to May, the name by which she was affectionately known long before she came to the Throne.

"A pretty child she was, with fair hair and blue eyes—very English looking," the Palace gatekeeper's wife said of her, remembering the child who was so inquisitive about the names of the flowers in the garden.

Princess May, as the future Queen Mary was known, had three brothers. At the time the Teck family were by no means wealthy. Because of a financial crisis they had to economise drastically. After a time Kensington Palace had to be given up, and then a period of exile in Italy was found necessary. For some eighteen months the Princess May studied in Florence under an Italian governess and had lessons from a painting master.

It was a time when women were emerging from their almost harem-like seclusion and acting and thinking for themselves. A quiet, sure revolution, with none of the hysterics and sensationalism which later was to be embodied in the Suffragette movement in Britain. Princess May was eager to develop her mental and intellectual qualities. She displayed an eager desire for knowledge. Helped by her Alsatian governess, Madame Bricka, she began a self-imposed task of six hours' serious reading each day. This decision was made in 1886, the year when she was seen on her appearance as a debutante.

Bricka, the Alsatian governess, was a

dominating character. She taught her young charge the importance of differentiating between the trivial and the important. The Empire owes much to that passionate, resolute, dark Alsatian woman, for Madame Bricka may be said to have moulded the character of our Queen.

Queen Mary has known what it is to be poor—really poor. When her father and mother lived at White Lodge, Richmond, they could not afford a carriage. Because it was the Victorian age and they were royalty, they had to have one. And so economies of the most stringent nature were absolutely necessary inside the house.

But Queen Victoria, with her passion for arranging the affairs of the House of Windsor, had already decided that Princess May should enter the royal circle. Under the watchful eye of the great Queen the young princess was encouraged to be studious, serious, and sedate. She was taught to read well and speak well.

Rumour said that she was shy and retiring, a contrast to the kindly, beloved, bustling Duchess of Teck, whom she often accompanied on philanthropic errands to the poor. She learnt the businesslike running of a household, getting a first-hand knowledge of that domestic art known as " making both ends meet."

Besides her course of serious reading, the future Queen studied music under Tosti, who found her an apt and amenable pupil. Her voice was a sweet but light soprano, which was unfortunately never heard outside the family circle.

But despite her life on the Continent and the opportunities she had of meeting many famous people, Princess May lived a life much different from that of the modern young woman on the Continent, drifting from Le Touquet to the Lido in a luxury cocktail tour. Her life was one of almost strict retirement.

This failure to extend her early circle of acquaintances may be due to the fact that all her life the Queen has not made friends easily. One of her best-informed biographers says: " In a less exalted circle, with fewer opportunities of coming into contact with every possible variety of temperament, she would probably have been a very lonely woman, but once she makes a friend, the friendship is a steadfast and enduring affection; she does not invite confidences, but in time of trouble she is a staunch and loyal supporter of those who have claims upon her."

Both Queen Victoria and the Princess of Wales (afterwards Queen Alexandra) developed a great affection and profound admiration for the reserved and beautiful daughter of the gay and debonair Duchess of Teck. She seemed marked out for greatness, and her engagement to the Duke of Clarence, the second in succession to the Throne, was received with no surprise, and, indeed, immense public enthusiasm.

This betrothal was announced in November, 1891. Then came the tragedy. The Duke died five weeks before the date of the wedding. Prince George, still convalescent from his own illness, became the heir-presumptive to the Throne.

The untimely death of the handsome young prince was looked upon as a national calamity. To Princess May it was a terrible blow. After the funeral she fled with her parents to White Lodge, Richmond, where she could think in quietness of the future and what it might have in store. Later she went to France with her mother to get over the blow. At the same time she did not forget the Princess of Wales, who was genuinely overcome with grief and sorrow over the death of her eldest son, for whom she had the deepest affection.

But, many months later, it was rumoured that Prince George was now paying court to the popular princess. There came the occasion when a family council was held at Windsor Castle to discuss the proposed marriage of Princess May and Prince George. Queen Victoria presided, and some shrewd comments were made by the subsequent King Edward VII.

Perhaps the preliminary tragedy of the death of the Duke of Clarence overshadowed and to some extent prevented the romantic courtship which the public delights upon in royal engagements. Nevertheless, when the future King asked her hand in marriage, Princess May replied: "I shall do my best to make you happy."

It cannot be said that she has failed. She has made herself the most dignified Queen in Europe, respected throughout the world. And her unswerving loyalty to England and its future has endeared her to all in the land.

There was genuine delight throughout the country when it was announced that the " Sailor Prince " had " made his own choice " and was to marry Princess May, a daughter of England. The engagement brought the congratulations of the Empire.

The Times expressed the popular feeling by saying: "We have the satisfaction of making the announcement for which the public will not be wholly unprepared. The understanding so long reported to exist between the Duke of York and Princess May has now taken the form of a definite betrothal, which has received the ready sanction of Her Majesty the Queen. We are certain that this intelligence will be received with sincere gratification.

" In the peculiar circumstances attending such a union, there must perforce be present in every mind a certain conflict of emotions. But the predominant feeling, now that a sufficient interval has elapsed since the melancholy death of the Duke of Clarence, will be that this betrothal accords with the fitness of things, and, so far from offending any legitimate sentiment, is the most appropriate and delicate medicament for the wound, in its nature, never wholly ineffaceable. There is even ground for hoping that a union rooted in painful memories may prove happy beyond the common lot. The persons of both parties are such as to attract sympathy. On the one hand, the Duke of York enjoys not only the popularity attaching to the Navy, but also a personal good will, founded on his own frank and manly bearing on the occasions when he has come before the public. The Princess May is endeared to the public by her personal charm and her amiable disposition, by the memory of her bereavement, and still more by the devotion she displayed at that trying juncture. . . ."

King Edward took control of the wedding arrangements, though they had, of course, to be approved by Queen Victoria. King Edward was a first-rate hand at arranging big ceremonials and enjoyed it.

The wedding ceremony was a splendid affair at the Chapel Royal, St. James's. Queen Victoria attended in full state, and every nation in the world sent either its monarch or heir to the

DO YOU REMEMBER THESE FASHIONS FOR SPORTSWOMEN? *It is hard to believe that less than twenty-five years ago women competitors in the Olympic Games were hampered by such voluminous garments. Compare them with the modern sports styles in other parts of this volume.*

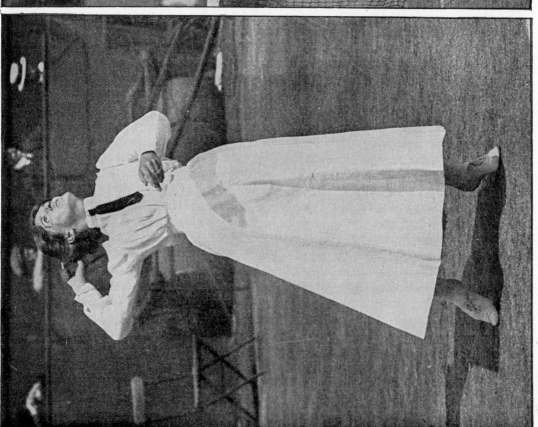

WHEN MRS. LAMBERT CHAMBERS *won the Ladies' Championship at Wimbledon before the war, her movements were hampered by prevailing fashions. Compare them with the simplicity and levity of the tennis girl's "shorts" in 1934. The player on the right is Mrs. Fearnley-Whittingstall, a pioneer of the new fashion.*

throne to do honour to the future King and Queen of England.

The Duke of Teck gave away his daughter. From the organ came the wedding march from *Lohengrin*. The Archbishop of Canterbury performed the ceremony, and Princess May had become the Duchess of York. At the end of it all a lone figure was seen leaning over a balcony railing in St. James's Palace, smoking a cigarette and looking rather forlorn. It was the Duke of Teck, father of the future Queen of England.

V

Once married, the Royal couple settled down to a life of quiet domesticity which, at the time, both desired, and which is still their desire to-day.

York House, in St. James's Palace, was a convenient and handsome residence in town, and York Cottage, if hardly a "stately domain," was sufficiently near to Sandringham House to be a welcome residence in Norfolk. It had served hitherto as an "overflow" annexe for those bachelor guests King Edward liked to have about him; but now it was to become rather a nursery than a guest house . . . so that, as Sir George Arthur has told us, our King ultimately was moved to exclaim: "I shall soon have a regiment, not a family."

The present Prince of Wales was born at White Lodge. The patron saints of England, Scotland, Ireland, and Wales were evoked at the baptism of the infant, who was destined to be the twentieth Prince of Wales, and for the first time in history a Queen Regnant held in her arms her descendant in the fourth generation.

It was little wonder that the birth of Edward Albert Christian George Andrew Patrick David was hailed with joy. Not since Tudor times, when Jane Seymour presented Henry VIII. with the sickly infant who was to become Edward VI., had an heir to the Throne been born in England of parents who gloried in their English birth.

The baptism was held in the Private Chapel at Windsor and was highly ceremonious. "Frock dress"—that is, knee-breeches and silk stockings, a uniform created by Prince Albert—was prescribed. The members of the Royal Family were gathered in force. Also many distinguished foreign guests. The Archbishop of Canterbury received the infant Prince, who, if carried by his nurse, was already attended by the Countess of Macclesfield. And a special choir broke into a chorale composed by the Prince Consort. "A trifle inappropriate," says Sir George Arthur, quoting the words:

In Life's gay morn, ere sprightly youth
By vice and folly is enslaved.

Apropos this baptism, we have recently had the story given by Lord Esher, Constable of Windsor. Lord Esher once sat next the future King George at dinner on the Royal yacht.

"He (George) mentioned a queer prophecy which he made me promise I would not repeat to the King (Edward), who is rather influenced by these old women's tales. Someone, about forty years ago, said of the late Queen that she would have a long and glorious reign, the longest and most glorious of all the English sovereigns; that she would be succeeded by two Kings who would have short reigns, and by a third whose name would be David, and whose name would be as glorious as hers. One of Prince Edward's names is David!

"When Lady Waterford was dying she sent for the Prince of Wales and implored him to call his then unborn son David, as she had some fad about restoring the Jews to the Holy City. To humour her, he consented, and Prince Edward was given the names of the four patron saints of England, Scotland, Ireland, and Wales—*i.e.*, George, Andrew, Patrick, David."

And that prophecy was twenty years or more before the British themselves went to Palestine!

Other children arrived. Five of Queen Mary's six children were born at York Cottage. And the future Queen Mary soon revealed herself as a devoted mother. She did her utmost to implant in her children her own love of reading and serious interest in art and literature. The Duke of York, however, seems to be the only one of her children who developed the studious habits of his mother.

This younger generation of the House of Hanover, as it was then, interested Lord Esher. He wrote in his diary:

"I was amused to-day by taking the Wales children, two boys and a girl, to the Abbey. They climbed on to every tomb and got very dirty, but were thoroughly happy. . . . Prince Edward remarked of the Duke of Buckingham that he was a 'wicked man,' and when I asked why, he said he gave bad advice to Charles I. He knew that Buckingham had been murdered at Portsmouth by Felton. I think he must have been reading Dumas!"

"The girl," of course, was Princess Mary, now Countess of Harewood.

Lord Esher could not help comparing "the boys" with each other. "The second boy," he wrote, "is the sharpest"—a nice compliment to the Duke of York—"but there is something rather taking about Prince Edward. He wants a walking-stick with a horse's head on it for his birthday."

The end of the great Queen Victoria was near. She was 80, and tired of all the pomp and circumstance. She excused herself from meeting her ministers. They would argue with her, and she would say, "You know I cannot any longer argue." Even her secretaries were kept at a distance. Ladies-in-waiting read the papers to her and brought down messages from her room which led to "complications."

She made a brave fight of it. At Netley Hospital there were two wounded soldiers to be decorated with the Victoria Cross. They were "sitting in chairs," and when the Queen was wheeled in "they were ordered to rise." But the Queen said, "Most certainly not." Without help—"a very unusual thing"—she raised herself "and stood over them while she decorated them."

*   *   *   *   *

So we come to the final drama, which must be described in Lord Esher's own words. This historic passage is as follows:

"The dying scene was stately and dramatic. The Queen now and then recognised those about her and spoke their names. Her difficulty in breathing was the only painful symptom. Reid—the doctor—passed his arm around her and supported her.

"The King knelt at the side of the bed. The German Emperor stood silently at the head, near the Queen. The other children and grandchildren were there, all calling their names to her

THE HEART OF THE
BRITISH EMPIRE,
1910-1934.

Piccadilly Circus has always been the heart of London, and is remembered with affection throughout the Empire. But even the Circus has changed with the times. Practically the only old landmark that remains is Eros, and even that has had a chequered career.

REGENT STREET,
1910-1934.

Remarkable changes have taken place in London's main shopping street. It was almost entirely rebuilt soon after the war.

at intervals. She died quite peacefully. After the King had left for London the Emperor took charge of everything, so unlike what was expected of him.

"He refused to allow Banting's men (the undertakers) to measure the Queen for her shell. He turned them out of the room. He sent for Reid, and took all the measurements himself. He and the King and the Duke of Connaught lifted the Queen into her coffin.

"The day before her death, while the Prince of Wales was in the house, but not allowed to go near the Queen for fear of alarming her, she said: 'The Prince of Wales will be sorry to hear how ill I am. Do you think he ought to be told?' Another thing she said was: 'I don't want to die yet. There are several things I want to arrange.'"

So ended the greatest reign in English history, and for a time all was confusion. People who ought to have known had forgotten the precedents to be followed.

At Windsor, Esher would see the Indian attendants of the dead Queen no longer "statuesque," but "wandering about like uneasy spirits"—and, if we may add a few details to the picture, what a housecleaning there had to be! An Oriental trophy in the Waterloo Gallery was touched—out flew a cloud of moths, and the trophy had to be burned in the courtyard. Tons of ivory, delivered as tribute by an African chief, were rotting in an attic. Huge supplies of plates with royal portraits on them, which had been intended to be given away as presents, were quietly disposed of. An immense paraphernalia of illuminated addresses, silver trowels, and other gifts had to be quietly obliterated.

Lord Esher felt the change from "the mystery and awe of the old court."

"Somehow," he wrote, "the sanctity of the Throne has disappeared." Dinner was served in the Edwardian style—not in the oak dining-room, but in a room all white—and "the quiet impressive entrance of the Queen into the corridor is as obsolete as Queen Elizabeth." Guests assembled in the green drawing-room and King Edward just walked in.

With King Edward's accession to the Throne a great change came to the household of Prince George and Mary. The real training of Prince George for the Kingship, which was to follow, now began.

Raised to the peerage as Duke of York, he was introduced in the House of Lords by his father. It was at that time he began the study of matters more closely related to the high office to which he was ultimately to be called—the working of the English Constitution and the various departments of public life— and he did it, as is his manner, with quiet, unostentatious, and thorough diligence.

During the ten years of the reign of King Edward, he was, as Prince of Wales, the companion and coadjutor of his father in the business of government. This was an experience which few Kings of England have had, although to-day the Prince of Wales does not hesitate to shoulder such burdens of State as come his way, and since the illness of King George, has relieved him of many tiring ceremonial duties.

The newly married couple, the Duke and Duchess of York, began an Empire tour soon after King Edward's accession to the Throne. The tour embraced India, Australia, New Zealand, South Africa, and Canada. They travelled over 50,000 miles, of which 38,000 were at sea.

Everywhere the Royal couple received a rapturous welcome. The moving experiences of a lifetime were packed into brief months. The Duke opened the first Parliament of Federated Australia at Melbourne; in New Zealand Maoris danced the War Poi-Poi dance before him and the Duchess; they ate the regulation lumberman's meal of soup, pork, beans, and hot, milkless tea, served in tin plates in a "combose" or lumberman's hut in Canada.

In a word, they entered thoroughly into almost every phase of Imperial life.

A pleasant musical incident occurred when the degree of LL.D. was conferred on the Duke at the Sydney University. The proceedings, as usual on these occasions, were uproarious, and the formalities preceding the presentation of degrees were more or less smothered by the singing of a special "anthem" composed for the occasion. It went to the tune of "A Life on the Ocean Wave," and the chorus ran thus:

> *Let every man with a voice*
> *His power of lung display;*
> *Yell loudly and rejoice,*
> *For the Jook is coming to-day;*
> *The Jook—the Jook—the Jook is coming*
>   *to-day.*
> *The Jook—the Jook—the Jook is coming*
>   *to-day.*

This breezy number amused the "Jook" very much.

During the *Ophir* tour the Duke shook hands with thirty-five thousand people, delivered nearly one hundred speeches, and distributed one hundred and forty titles. The brain reels at this endless procession of civic receptions, laying of foundation stones, opening of buildings, and other functions. But the Duke went through it all with a cheery smile and a kind word for everyone.

It was on his return home in March, 1902, that the Duke was made Prince of Wales. Speaking at a luncheon given at the Guildhall by the Lord Mayor and Corporation, he said:

"If I were asked to specify any particular impressions derived from our tour I should unhesitatingly place before all others those of loyalty to the Crown and attachment to the old country."

It was on this occasion that he delivered a memorable exhortation: "Wake up, England!" It was a call for settlers for the "boundless tracts of country yet unexplored, hidden mineral wealth calling for development; vast expanses of virgin soil ready to yield profitable crops."

But Destiny was hurrying on apace. Came that day in May, 1910, when King Edward realised that his reign was at an end. The eyes of the world, and particularly of England, were centred upon his son Prince George. And the future Queen Mary was with her husband in those dark hours which saw the end of one reign and the beginning of another.

And so they stood beside a dead king, these characters who were on the stage for twenty-five years of incredible and dramatic happenings. Not even the shrewd King Edward realised the cataclysm that these twenty-five years were to see upthrust. And even those who gathered about the death-bed of the King might well have quailed at the task before them if they had but known.

CHAPTER II

ENGLAND IN 1910

Revolution in Europe—Quarrel between the House of Lords and House of Commons—Demand for prison reform—Wireless and crime—Lily Elsie and Gertie Millar, the " toasts " of London—Popular Marie Lloyd.

I

THE year 1910, twelve months before the official Coronation of King George V., opened ominously for royalty. There arrived on these shores the first of those royal exiles, the first king to lose his throne in an era that was to see half the thrones of Europe totter and fall.

Revolution had broken out in Portugal. As usual, the first act of the revolutionaries was to cut the cable between Lisbon and England, and for some days no news came through. Nobody could say what had happened to the young King Manoel, although it was rumoured he had escaped. Pessimists, however, recalled that two years previously King Carlos and the Crown Prince of Portugal had been shot while driving through the streets of Lisbon. It seemed certain that a similar fate awaited the young King Manoel at the hands of the desperate revolutionaries.

But in a few days the veil of silence was lifted. The special correspondents of the newspapers who had reached Lisbon began to send their dramatic messages. It was then learned that the secret, revolutionary societies had planned a *coup d'état* and been successful. King Manoel had escaped from the palace and been taken aboard a British warship.

By the time Manoel reached England it was obvious that Portugal intended to be a Republic. There was practically no chance of regaining the throne. Manoel accepted the situation philosophically. He settled down to the life of a country gentleman in England, with an income that caused him no immediate worries. He appeared in Mayfair, attended many public ceremonies, and in his later years was able to watch the debacle of the Great War sweeping over Europe and carrying with it many a royal throne.

But the new King of England was faced with a revolution which was taking place in the political world bounded by Westminster. It was the long constitutional battle between the House of Lords and the House of Commons, now coming to a head. The struggle had reached its intensity with the Budget of 1909. Mr. Asquith, as Prime Minister, warned the House of Lords that if the Budget was rejected he would demand Royal authority for a sufficient creation of peers to make the passing of Government Bills a certainty.

The death of King Edward had shaken the protagonists in this duel. Was there not then possibility of compromise? Men gossiped of what might well have happened if the King had lived and again called the leaders to conference. There was at any rate this ground for such speculation, that King

Edward was fairly well known to have used what influence he could within his marked discretion to prevent the precipitation, by the rejection of the Budget, of a struggle which he deplored as bad politics.

There was a distinct sigh of relief throughout the country when it was announced that a conference was to meet, composed of Mr. Asquith, Lord Crewe, Mr. Lloyd George, and Mr. Birrell on the one side, and Mr. Balfour, Lord Lansdowne, Lord Cawdor, and Mr. Austen Chamberlain on the other. It began its meetings in June.

At the same time there was a sudden demand throughout the country for prison reform. Critics of the system were suggesting that our prisons were still in the torturous atmosphere of the Middle Ages. Worst of all was the solitary confinement system.

This growing criticism was helped by the staging of a new play by John Galsworthy. The play, *Justice*, depicted a clerk condemned to solitary confinement. The wordless scene in which he is alone in his cell, pacing to and fro, and suddenly flings himself at the door, pounding madly with his fists, gave a thrill of horror to the well-dressed audience that filled the theatre nightly. The climax of the play, in which the convict on ticket-of-leave kills himself in sheer despair, added to the moral urgency of the theme.

Mr. Winston Churchill was Home Secretary at the time. He faced the clamour, and agreed that reform was necessary. He admitted, too, that Mr. Galsworthy's picture was not overdrawn, and that he had himself been moved by seeing the play. As a result, there began that series of reforms in prison life which have now reached a decent, humanitarian stage. Lectures and concerts were begun in prisons. The Borstal system was extended by the opening of a new institution at Feltham.

Wireless, too, came to the public notice in a sensational fashion. For some days police and Press had been indulging in a great manhunt for a missing Dr. Crippen, the murdered remains of whose wife had been discovered in the cellar of a house in Camden Town. This may be said to be the first occasion on which the Press entered upon a murder hunt in the full clamour of startling headlines and graphic, if gruesome, details.

But it was wireless that brought the hunted man to justice. The newspapers published the amazing news that the captain of a steamer on the way to Canada had sent a wireless message stating that he believed the missing man and his companion were on board. With their usual enterprise the *Daily Mail* began a series of wireless day-by-day stories with the captain of the ship, giving details of the daily life aboard of the couple. At the same time a Scotland Yard detective hurried by a faster steamer to Canada to head off the fugitives. Oblivious of the newspaper clamour and the cackling wireless above their heads, the couple believed themselves safe from detection.

Crippen was arrested and condemned to death. But the sordid details of the crime were lost in the public's dawning appreciation of the dramatic importance that wireless was going to play in their lives. For the moment broadcasting was unknown, although such brilliant brains as Marconi were toying with the idea. Wireless in 1910 was just a series of faint Morse messages between ships, likely to be useful in case of impending

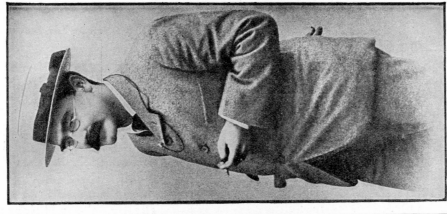

RUDYARD KIPLING *was the great literary figure of the day. His short stories and poems about the Empire appealed strongly to the Imperialists.*

LILY ELSIE *was at this time toasted as Britain's most beautiful actress.*

THE FIRST ALEXANDRA ROSE DAY, *inaugurated by Queen Alexandra, was held on June 21, 1912. This flag day is still maintained.*

disaster. It was a safety invention, with a dominant S.O.S. *motif*.

For the most part, however, England, and London in particular, found itself comfortable, rich, and secure. The Edwardian age had seen gay and frolicsome parties. They would continue into the reign of the new King. The world looked good to the middle-aged of those days. The Empire was prosperous. True, there were mutterings beneath the surface. The trades union movement was making itself felt, and entering the Law Courts to contest charges of illegality. A lean caballero in frock coat and top-hat, Mr. Cunninghame Graham stood on the plinth in Trafalgar Square and talked to workless men of the benefits of Socialism. And strange, strident women were appearing with an unreasonable demand for the vote. "Suffragettes" they were called, contemptuously.

But the solid Londoner ignored these storm mutterings. He was being driven with his family in one of the new-fangled taxicabs to His Majesty's Theatre in the Haymarket, where Sir Herbert Tree was displaying a lavish production of *Henry VIII*. But not "The Private Life of Henry VIII." It was Shakespeare's rather tame history made flamboyant and exciting by one of the most colourful theatrical figures that ever walked the London stage.

Musical comedy, too, essentially an English product, was at the height of its glory. *The Merry Widow* waltz and hat had swept the country, and the latest production of Oscar Strauss, *The Chocolate Soldier*, was then being performed for the first time.

It was the day of Lily Elsie and Gertie Millar. Their smiling faces stared at adoring youth from the glazed picture-postcards, the collection of which was the craze of the moment. When the English composer, Lionel Monckton, produced *The Quaker Girl* at the Adelphi with his wife, Gertie Millar, now the Countess of Dudley, in the leading part, the whole of London and the provinces flocked to hear the tuneful music and cheer the beauty of the Quaker Girl herself.

Daly's Theatre, the real home of musical comedy, countered with *The Dollar Princess*. Lily Elsie played the lead in this production, and began that series of tremendous successes which continued up to the days of the Great War.

For those who demanded even lighter entertainment there was a huge clown, with white face and pierrot's costume, one Pélissier, who presented his group known as "The Follies." They acted in farcical fashion a series of "Potted Plays." One first-night reception was hardly successful. The audience booed loudly at the fall of the curtain. But the curtain went up again to reveal the bulky Pélissier booing back at the audience.

And the first Russian ballets were exciting London. It was the time when Pavlova could be seen sinking gracefully to the stage, a lovely dying swan, to the music of Saint-Saëns. Mayfair, too, was being shocked in drawing-rooms by the dancing of Maud Allen, whose dramatic interpretation of *Salomé* raised a theatrical storm of the first order.

The cinema was practically unknown. Electricity was only just taking the place of gas for footlights. Eros, in Piccadilly Circus, stood on solid earth and not upon a series of lighted caves where electric trains rumbled. The West End was a luxury city. The clubs in Pall

Mall were the most exclusive in the world. To walk along Piccadilly was to feel oneself in the finest street of the greatest city in the world.

But the real home of entertainment for the people was the music-hall. It was, at the moment, freeing itself from that public-house atmosphere in which it really began. Its songs and people were racy and of the soil. It scorned the pretentiousness in life, and laughed at its own vulgarity, at its mothers-in-law, its West End drinks, its marital adventurers.

These were the days of giants in the music-hall. Cinquevalli, the greatest genius in balancing billiard balls and even billiard tables that the world has ever seen. It was the day of great tricksters on the stage. Chung Ling Soo, that almond-eyed, pigtailed conjurer who in reality hailed from Lancashire. The great Lafayette, the mammoth illusionist to whom, even in these days of mammoth shows, Mr. Bertram Mills might respectfully doff his hat. Twice nightly, and sometimes thrice nightly, these self-styled "artistes" amused the working world of England from Tyneside to Shoreditch.

It was the era of great comedians. George Formby, the consumptive lad from Lancashire. What a shout of laughter would rise as the sour-faced, rough-voiced comedian in the check suit too small for him staggered on the stage and nodded to "George" the conductor. And when he burst into that dry tremolo song:

"*I was standing at the corner of the street . . .*"

there would be thunderous applause at the finish.

Another northern comedian, Harry Weldon, had his own enthusiastic audience. Harry Weldon keeping goal! Stiffy, a football fool in a million. And Stiffy, the boxer, introduced by his comic manager, offering to fight " . . . any lady . . . any lady?" If a member of the audience showed a disposition to tackle the fighter on the stage, Stiffy would implore his manager to "tell 'em what I did to Colin Bell!" Thus, many a second encounter was avoided.

It was the day, too, when Harry Tate's moustache, twisting across his face, was becoming known to millions. The fishing episode, the motoring catastrophe—they rocked with laughter, those glittering halls, from the Five Towns to the sweaty atmosphere of Glasgow music-halls.

"Harry" was a generous name among comedians of that time. Harry Lauder was then emerging from his life as a miner to the top-liner in music-hall bills all over the Empire. But what the Empire in Leicester Square enjoyed to-day, the Empire beyond the sea would enjoy to-morrow. That crooked, knobby stick carried by the crooked, knobby figure of the man in tartan plaid, the raucous Scottish voice rolling forth:

"*Oh, stop yer ticklin', Jock!*"

even a wilderness of modern talkie films could not give the same zest as the audiences in those days received.

And the women of the music-halls! Can their like be found in the flat-chested sylphs of to-day's musical films? For the most part they were generous in figure, even if they only displayed legs as "principal boys" in Christmas pantomime. They had the hearts of millions of Englishmen before Mae West.

Chief among them was Marie Lloyd. Born at Hoxton, she staggered beneath the names of Matilda Alice Victoria. But to all the Cockney world until she died she was Marie Lloyd. Her two greatest songs, perhaps, which achieved world-wide renown for her are: "I'm One of the Ruins that Cromwell knocked abaht a Bit," and another whose chorus ran:

> "My old man
> Said 'Follow the van,
> Don't dilly-dally on the w'y!'
> Orf went the van
> With the old man in it;
> I walked behind
> With my old cock linnet.
> I dallied and dillied,
> And dillied and dallied,
> Lorst my w'y and don't know
>   where to roam,
> 'Cos you can't trust the speshuls
>   like the old-time coppers,
> When you can't find your way
>   home."

Marie Lloyd was at her zenith in these early Georgian days. At the time when the Oxford, London Pavilion, and Tivoli were the leading music-halls in London, Marie would be appearing at all three, booked for months on end. Her times would be:

Oxford	... ...	9.40
Pavilion	... ...	10.10
Tivoli	... ...	10.35

Her admirers used to go from one hall to the other to enjoy over and over again a performance which was frequently identical. These houses were one-show-a-night halls, and she used to fit in a suburban music-hall as well.

Marie Lloyd was three times married, "with varying unhappiness." During the Great War she sang again and again to wounded men, and brought some little brightness into those drab and tragic days.

Her own end was in itself a stage tragedy. She collapsed on the stage of the Edmonton Empire while singing her character song: "I'm One of the Ruins that Cromwell knocked abaht a Bit." When she swayed about on the stage in the song the audience thought she was realistically imitating a drunken woman; but actually she could have had little idea of what she was doing.

Perhaps the finest tribute to her art is that by Mr. James Agate, the famous dramatic critic.

"When in the Tottenham Court Road I saw, tucked under the newsboy's arm, the sheet which announced that Marie Lloyd was dead," he wrote, "everything around me became still. The street lost its hubbub, and for a space I was alone with a personal sorrow. . . .

"'Marie'—pronounced with the broad vowel beloved of the Cockney—was in everybody's mouth that day, in club and barrack-room, in bar parlour and in modest home. On the high seas 'Marie's dead' would be droned from ship to ship. Returning from Kempton a party of bookmakers fell to speaking of the dead artist. One said, with tears in his eyes, 'She had a heart, had Marie!' 'The size of Waterloo Station,' another rejoined.

"Her abounding generosity was a commonplace of the profession. She would go down to Hoxton, where she was born and make lavish distribution to the street-urchins of boots and shoes which she fitted with her own hands. She had numberless pensioners dependent upon her charity. She earned some two hundred thousand pounds and gave it all away. 'God rest her,' said the bookmaker who had first spoken, and

She spent a great deal of time entertaining soldiers who had been permanently disabled.

DEATH OF MARIE LLOYD.

The death of Marie Lloyd, the great Cockney comedienne, on October 7, 1922, came as a great shock to the English people. She was only 52, and had been appearing on the stage for 37 years. Her most famous songs were "Oh, Mr. Porter, Whatever Shall I do?" and "I Do Like to be Beside the Seaside." Thousands of Londoners were present at her funeral.

The companies agreed to call in all their old films and burn them. Then they began afresh on the present renting system. The photograph above shows a bonfire of Selig films.

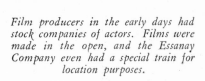

Film producers in the early days had stock companies of actors. Films were made in the open, and the Essanay Company even had a special train for location purposes.

DINORBEN ARMS

Photos: By courtesy of Will Day, Esq.

bared his head. That night, at Black-friars Ring, a bruiser with the marks of many fights declared: "We shan't none of us see the likes o' Marie again. She wur a great artist! . . ."

What a contrast to the Hollywood film stars of today! These artists of the old music-hall were flesh and blood, not creatures in a shadow-show or enticing covers to film fan magazines. They lived among the people, and made the people laugh and cry.

So one of the same group was Vesta Tilley, the first great female impersonator. In those days she was strutting the stage in male evening-dress, topper at the back of her close-cropped head, and singing about the Johnnies of the West End. There was Happy Fanny Fields, a Dutch girl in wooden clogs and with an infectious laugh.

The films, in fact, had hardly begun in those days. True, on the music-hall stage of the time was a little Cockney boy from Walworth, who sang with the Eight Lancashire Lads, and later on acted with the comedians who did acrobatic feats in Fred Karno's sketch, *The Mumming Birds*. His name was Charles Spencer Chaplin, and few people dreamed that in a few years he would be the most celebrated shadow comedian in the history of the world.

The only pictures which the public saw were those little boxes on pedestals in derelict shops. The box was called a mutoscope, and those who slipped a penny in the slot and looked through the slot could see a number of photographs whirled round so rapidly that the figures in the photographs appeared to be moving.

"The novelty of the mutoscope," writes Mr. St. John Ervine, "did not make it popular except among youths like myself, who, profoundly stirred by the information that if they dropped a penny in the slot they would see moving pictures of a young lady undressing, squandered large sums on disappointing exhibitions. For immediately after the lady had removed her blouse the light went out. Hollywood has learnt a lot since the days of the mutoscope."

Nevertheless, moving-pictures had definitely arrived. There were strange, shed-like contraptions fitted out like railway coaches. Seated inside the audience were given a photographic representation of a railway journey, and to add to the effect the coach was jolted slightly.

And, in the wilds of Twickenham, Chrissie White and Henry Edwards were already Britain's first film stars, producing a series of comedies which might to-day provoke mirth of another kind. But for the most part, no one paid attention to the queer people who were busy with moving-pictures, except, on occasions, to complain of their disastrous activities; for on January 11, 1908, there was a panic at a cinematograph exhibition in Barnsley, and sixteen children were killed, and two days later a cinematograph exploded at Boyestown, Pennsylvania, and more than 160 persons were killed.

The legitimate theatre was still triumphing, though a tremendous revolution was taking place there. The old theatrical stars who were content with any sort of play, providing that it gave them a good rousing theatrical speech and plenty of limelight, found themselves confronted by a group of playwrights with extraordinary ideas on what constituted a play.

It had all begun with a fellow named Ibsen, a Scandinavian who wrote most depressing plays. Modern playwrights were actually enthusiastic about Ibsen, and insisted upon writing plays in the same manner. Pinero, Henry Arthur Jones, Bernard Shaw, J. M. Barrie, John Galsworthy, and Harley Granville-Barker were calmly insisting that their plays were the plays of the future. Moreover, they were actually introducing bedsteads on to the stage, and not for farcical reasons either. Old "laddies" meeting at the Bodega shook their heads and declared that the theatre was "going to the dogs, old boy."

There was a night when a gentleman under the influence of liquor lurched into the Theatre Royal in Dublin during the performance of a play by Mr. Shaw. He sat, in some dismay, through three acts, and then, unable to bear the play any longer, cried out in a voice husky with drink and indignation, "D'you call this a play? Lasht time I was here I saw a fat fella and a tall, thin fella slapping him in the stummick wid a walkin' stick. That was a grand play. . . ."

None of these fierce critics and public protesters realised that somewhere in the sunshine wastes of California a group of men were getting together, who, with their cameras and their shadow artists, would completely transform the entertainment tastes of the world.

II

Another new era was opening, this time in the sky. Adventurous men in Norfolk jackets were attempting queer things in the air with glorified kites.

True, the public had heard of these things, but they were not taken too seriously. The Americans, Wilbur Wright and his brother, had been experimenting with their flying machines in France.

The Wrights were the real pioneers of flight. Their machine was, of course, made at Dayton, Ohio. It was a biplane with, in front, two small planes which served as elevator control, and two vertical planes behind for rudder. Its four-cylinder engine was of twenty-four horse-power, and was connected by chains to two wooden propellers.

It was not fashioned on wheels, as is the 'plane of to-day, but on skids like a sleigh, so that after each flight it had to be dragged back to an odd-looking device of spring-boards with a super catapult attachment. Then at the proper moment, with engine running, the 'plane all set and Wright aboard, the lever was pulled, the catapult did its job, and up went the 'plane.

But flying was already being discussed with enthusiasm by a little group in England. Very soon actual flights were being made. And, as seems natural in this country, the pioneer aviators started by breaking the law.

As recently as 1909 it was a punishable offence to fly, or rather to attempt to do so, except within certain hours. When in that year Mr. A. V. Roe, later Sir Alliott Roe, made his first flight he was followed ruthlessly by the police, who took his name and address. Before the case could come to court, however, the law was dramatically amended by M. Bleriot's flight across the Channel.

The twenty-fifth anniversary of this sensational flight was recently celebrated by the flight of a young Englishman across the Channel upside down. But Bleriot himself is still alive and the story of his flight is still an amazing adventure.

"One fine morning I took off from the village of Sangalle on the cliffs of Picardy at dawn," says Bleriot. "There was hardly any wind. I had no compass, meteorology was not organised as is the case to-day, to supply aviators with essential information, and I had to steer by sight. The engine revolved regularly and without knocking. During the first minutes I saw behind me the white track of the torpedo-boat destroyer which Latham had lent me and which was trying to follow me in order to render assistance in case of need. But the boat went much less quickly than I, and I soon lost sight of her.

"Everything went smoothly, visibility was perfect and I had just caught sight of the cliffs of Dover when I was suddenly enveloped in fog. A most uncomfortable ten minutes followed. I was out of sight of the French coast and the English coast was still a long way off. If I should fall into the sea—which was extremely likely—I did not think I could get out again, as I was still a cripple as the result of a crash at Douai a few weeks before.

"In the fog I had drifted north of Dover, and had to fly in a wide circle to get back on my course. The morning mist dispersed; the sun shone brilliantly. Once more I saw the chalk cliffs flashing and the fields of the impregnable island. . . .

"Was victory assured?

"Three times I tried to land on the cliffs, and three times the machine refused to climb so high. I swung her round in desperation, happy to find that in spite of all that had been required of her she continued to throb regularly.

"At last I found a cliff near Dover lower than those which had defeated me before, and there I made an easy landing.

"The Channel was crossed."

The conquest of the English Channel by Bleriot brings us to the contentious subject with which I opened. Who was the first Englishman to fly? In 1908 an American, S. F. Cody, was making flights in England and soon A. V. Roe was doing likewise. In 1928 the Royal Aero Club tried to solve this problem. They appointed a committee to determine who was the first British subject to fly in a heavier-than-air machine in the British Isles.

After considering a variety of evidence, the committee decided that this distinction had been achieved by Lieut.-Col. J. T. C. Moore-Brabazon, at Leysdown, near Eastchurch in the Isle of Sheppey, between April 30 and May 2, 1909. On this occasion he flew a distance of between a quarter and half a mile at a height of from fifty to eighty feet.

The flights of A. V. Roe, made at Brooklands, were considered, but the committee decided that these were in the nature of hops and not official flights. Nevertheless, it was those early exploits of A. V. Roe that helped to build up the great industry of British aviation.

Among the other pioneers of those days in England were Handley-Page, Sopwith, de Havilland, Short and Blackburn. All of them helped in the development of British aviation and all have their machines flying the skyways of to-day.

It was the period, too, when the *Daily Mail*, under Lord Northcliffe's inspired guidance, began that series of gigantic money prizes for successful flights in this country. But for the most part the public were content to look up to the sky from the earth and not down at the earth from a machine. As an invention, the flying machine was considered too hazardous to be taken seriously.

There was the great race between London and Manchester, for the accomplishment of which within 24 hours the *Daily Mail* had offered £10,000. There were two serious competitors, Paulhan, a Frenchman, and our own Grahame-White.

There was a private agreement between the two airmen that they would give each other due notice when they were ready to start. But at six o'clock one evening Grahame-White learned that Paulhan had started from Hendon and got clear away with an hour's start.

Grahame-White determined to follow. Although the sun was setting and night flying in those days was an extremely hazardous business, the Englishman was not deterred. In a series of two exciting hops he reached the Midlands before midnight, his mother and sister following, desperately anxious, in a car. But at his second forced landing he learned that Paulhan had reached Manchester, and thereby won the £10,000 prize.

"The best man has won" was his sporting comment when the news came to him. Later Grahame-White with his aeroplanes was to make real history in the aviation world.

Not long after, these adventurous fellows of the air actually arranged an aviation meeting at Bournemouth in 1910. And the public shook its head sadly, but wisely, when the meeting was marred by the death of the Hon. C. S. Rolls, of the famous Rolls Royce car firm. This young man crashed in the sea.

The price paid by these early pioneers was high. There were thirty-three deaths during 1910, the total since the beginning of aviation being thus brought up to forty-two; sixty-five in 1911; ninety-five in 1912—the numbers mounted steadily. To the public, indeed, the progress of aeronautics was marked by a succession of spectacular feats of flight, punctuated by sudden death. To the inventor it was the gradual evolution of means to an end: the ultimate discovery of a machine which would combine all the requirements of an aerial conveyance with safety.

Flying over the sea at this time was considered a most daring feat; no one ever contemplated that the Atlantic could be flown. A fourth crossing of the Channel, this time by a Mr. Moisant, an American, and a flight by Robert Loraine, the actor, to Ireland in September, were enthusiastically described by the newspapers, as were also the facts that Loraine had flown on one occasion in a storm, and that another aviator had attained a speed in the air of some 75 to 95 miles an hour.

Airships, too, were still considered to be competing with aeroplanes for the future of flying. Mr. Willows flew a small dirigible from Cardiff to London, and later flew it round St. Paul's, by way of demonstrating its possibilities as a "one-man" rival to the 'plane.

In the meantime, an old man, by the name of Count Zeppelin, was experimenting in the construction of a rigid type of airship at Friedrichshafen on Lake Constance. Already four Zeppelins had been launched, the last perishing in flames as a result of being struck by lightning.

The disaster, in which happily no one was killed, seemed to have ended the experiments of the old inventor. To help him construct new airships subscriptions were raised all over the world. France, the United States, and Great

GRAHAME-WHITE *was one of Britain's pioneer airmen. He took part in the famous* 1910
*London to Manchester air race, which he lost, and later was to make history in the
aviation world.*

Britain vied in generosity with his own country. Ironically, Britain did not realise that these same airships, over which the people were so enthusiastic, would in a few years be bombing London and the provincial towns.

But Count Zeppelin himself had fully realised the military value of his invention. He announced that he had placed his invention at the disposal of his own countrymen. The German Government presented him with a grant of half a million marks, and the subscriptions received from abroad were politely returned.

Further Zeppelins were built, each improved in various details and equipped with motors of greater power than its predecessor. So convincingly did they demonstrate the reliability of this type of aircraft that regular airship transport services were begun in Germany. At the time of the outbreak of the war in 1914 provincial airship travel was well established in that country.

But Britain was not entirely neglecting airships. Elongated balloons, not intended for long flights, but rather for surveying military operations, were being tested. The first British airship, built in 1907 at the Royal Aircraft Establishment at Farnborough, was of this type. Subsequently several other non-rigid airships were built or purchased by the Army authorities, but they were not very successful.

The *Beta,* a non-rigid airship of 35,000 cubic feet capacity, performed good work between 1910 and 1912 and on one of her flights flew from Farnborough to London and back.

The *Gamma* (capacity 75,000 cubic feet) had a speed of 28 miles an hour.

The *Delta,* also a non-rigid airship, with a capacity of 180,000 cubic feet, and a lifting force of $5\frac{1}{2}$ tons, was completed in 1912. She was capable of a maximum speed of 45 miles an hour, with a range of 350 miles.

The *Delta* is notable for the fact that from it wireless telegraphy transmissions were successfully carried out, and on another occasion a parachute descent was safely accomplished.

The first rigid airship to be built in Great Britain was constructed in 1911 by Vickers, Ltd. It was built for the Admiralty, and was known variously as the *Mayfly,* and " Naval Airship No. 1." The *Mayfly* represented much thought and money, but its career was of short duration, for it was wrecked while being taken out of its hangar at Barrow-in-Furness.

And, as we shall see through the succeeding pages of this twenty-five years of history, ill-luck and terrible tragedy dogged all the British attempts in airship construction.

Nevertheless, in this year of 1910, men were beginning to lift their eyes to the skies; there were enthusiasts who envisaged the new air arm as the dominant factor in military and naval operations, while others saw the beginnings of air transport and passenger lines throughout the world. A great mechanical awakening, to which the pulses of men stirred.

But there was no doubt in the minds of the public regarding the great future of the motor-car. Although still a novelty on the English roads, supreme confidence had caused the building of Brooklands Track as early as 1906. Motor-racing was considered to be the great sport of the future.

It is strange to think that the familiar taxi-cab was not seen on the streets of London until 1904; and then there were only three of them, called motor-hansoms. Two had 12-horse-power Herald engines, and the third was a 6-horse-power single-cylinder De Dion. They were driven by cabmen specially trained for the work, and these men were required to bring in ten pounds a week. They sometimes made five pounds in a day. Officers going back to Aldershot were their special patrons.

The old hansom-drivers hated the new taxis. "Stinking steam-kettle" was the mildest term they used. The public, on the contrary, loved them, and they increased so rapidly that within four years there were two million pounds' worth of them running in London and another three hundred on order. Even so, London was still a long way behind Paris, where there were already 4,000 taxi-cabs.

The first London taxis charged eight-pence a mile, and relied on the old printed list of distances to calculate their fares. In 1906 the taximeter came into use, and for the first time the passenger knew exactly the legal fare for any distance.

The charge at the time was sixpence a mile. The change was a popular one, for the drivers who had previously paid ten shillings a day to the cab-owners were now entitled to keep one-third of the takings.

Arrangements were made to train a number of the old horse-cab drivers in the driving of motors. They received a month's training, during which they were paid a pound a week, and in return they signed a contract to work for the motor-cab company for two years.

By 1908 there were 758 taxi-cabs on the streets of London and 2,600 more on order. New drivers were coming in so rapidly that fifty-five certificates were issued each week. Within the next two years the number of motor-cabs had increased to 5,070. The taxis of those days had quite comfortable bodies, but the engines were small, usually only 8 to 10 horse-power. Their cost averaged £350 and the weekly takings of each cab about £16.

In this year of 1910 the last horse-drawn omnibus ran its final journey from London Bridge. London was to know no more that cheery, red-faced individual with a whip and a Cockney wit, both of which generously flashed. In his place came the mechanic at the wheel, the forerunner of that marvellous strategist of the London streets whom we know to-day.

The London General Omnibus Company had been early in the field applying the internal combustion engine to road transport. It began with a petrol-electric vehicle on the streets in 1903, and in 1904 the first horseless omnibus began to ply between Hammersmith and Piccadilly.

For some years a war raged between petrol, steam, and electric buses. They were all on the streets at once. The electro bus was by far the quieter and more pleasant vehicle in which to travel, but the weight of the accumulators killed it as a paying proposition. These weighed from thirteen to twenty hundredweight as compared with a hundred pounds' weight of petrol for a petrol-driven vehicle of similar carrying power.

Eventually the petrol bus triumphed, and the L.G.O.C. devoted its energies to constantly improving its rapidly increasing service. Between 1910 and 1911 its drivers and conductors were provided with a uniform, and motor-omnibus services began to run to the country on Sundays and Bank Holidays. Epping Forest was the first resort to be visited by bus, and thousands of Londoners took advantage of the cheap fares to get out of the streets into the country. These new outings proved so popular that by 1912 services were running to Windsor, St. Albans, Watford, Farnborough, and Sidcup, and in the following year to Reigate, Caterham, and Dorking. There were as yet no motor coaches. These were a post-war development.

The transformation of London's tramways from horse-drawn to electrically-driven vehicles was also complete. They were extending their wires and rails even further into the suburbs. The running of the tramway along the Embankment in 1906, and the opening of the tram subway under Kingsway in 1908, at last linked up the systems serving north and south London. The tramways of the provinces emulated those of the capital in their adoption of electricity as motive power.

The old and dirty "Tuppenny Tube" had also gone. The Underground Electric Railways Company had been formed, and they proceeded to electrify and extend their services. The Piccadilly tube, between Hammersmith and Finsbury Park, had been completed in 1906. The year following Mr. Lloyd George, then President of the Board of Trade, opened the Hampstead, Highgate, and Charing Cross tube. Passengers were carried free on the opening day, and some 127,500 availed themselves of this privilege. London, it will be observed, was beginning to sprawl into that huge cosmopolis that we know to-day.

This, too, was the era of the turbine and the monster liner. In 1907 the *Lusitania* and the *Mauretania*, sister ships, unprecedented floating towns of 31,500 tons apiece, were launched. Even bigger ships for the Atlantic route were demanded. The challenge of the Cunard Company was countered by the White Star Line in 1910 by the launching of the *Olympic*. And a few feet away, in the same shipyard, the ill-fated *Titanic* was being constructed.

Both the *Lusitania* and the *Titanic* were to become symbols of great international tragedy—the one bringing the United States alongside Britain in the war against Germany, the other producing a common bond of sorrow between the relatives of the drowned in this country and America.

But of all these great liners that marked British shipbuilding at its best, the *Mauretania*, only just withdrawn from the Atlantic ferry, has the outstanding record of service.

Built in 1907, she was, before the Great War, a wonder of the western ocean. To cross in this fast ship was rightly regarded as a remarkable experience. During the war she was of great value to the nation, and she was called upon to render, in turn, various vital services. After the war she returned to her regular routes of peace-time and she continued to make the fastest passage across the ocean.

The work which she has performed over a long period is a tribute to the designers and builders of the ship and her engines. To steam across the North Atlantic in all weathers at high speed involves a strain on hull and machinery which, in the course of time, must tell, and only a very finely built ship could have lasted as she has done, and have seemed for years to possess the qualities of youth.

A catch phrase was dominating the construction of battleships in Britain. "We want eight and we won't wait!" was the slogan that began the building of those super-dreadnoughts, the marvels of modern naval construction. In 1909 the *Colossus* was launched on the Clyde, and the *Orion* at Portsmouth, more than 40,000 people witnessing the latter ceremony. The year after three super-dreadnoughts, including the *Thunderer*, at which the wife of the Archbishop of Canterbury officiated, were launched.

The gigantic race in naval armaments with Germany had begun. Naval experts believed, triumphantly, that the dreadnought was the last word in supremacy of the seas. They did not foresee—neither did the Germans for that matter—that these floating steel fortresses would really reduce war at sea to a stalemate, just as the increasing mechanisation of armies would make a mobile war almost impossible. During the Great War these super-dreadnoughts revealed themselves as being at the mercy of any chance floating mine or the undersea torpedo launched by a submarine.

But as they slid down the stocks in the year 1910 and were launched in a furore of excitement, everybody sincerely believed that Britannia really ruled the waves.

III

Not only was this the period of limelight stars of whom we are told "the like will never be seen again," but it was also the age of literary giants.

Bernard Shaw, H. G. Wells, Arnold Bennett, James Barrie, George Moore, and Thomas Hardy—they had each helped to place England on the literary map of the world.

It was the era, too, of the new journalism. Pearson, Newnes, and Harmsworth were a trinity of men who were achieving astounding success with periodicals that frankly catered for the million.

And the writers of those days enjoyed the full tide of that popular journalism, with its high prices and good reading. It is doubtful whether the short story, as one example, has ever risen to the heights maintained by the writers of those days.

Still firmly established at the head of this school was Rudyard Kipling. His jingling verse, with its imperialistic theme, appealed strongly to a country that had come through the Boer War victorious, but slightly ashamed of itself.

The short stories of Kipling, with their insistence upon the romance of "the day's work," were read widely from Sydney to Grimsby, from Cape Town to Hong Kong, and from Toronto to Calcutta. Heroes in mechanics' overalls; swearing, blasphemous, but heroic figures in khaki; sun-stewed men of the tropics; salt-stained men of the seven seas—these were the characters who stamped and tramped their way through the pages of Rudyard Kipling, and even the Little Englander of those days was shaken from his beliefs by these sagas of the men who had taken up "the white man's burden."

About the same time, Mr. Arnold Bennett was religiously writing in that famous diary:

"*After several days' delay, owing to indisposition, I began to write 'Hilda Lessways' yesterday afternoon; only 400 words. To-day 1,100 words. It seems to be a goodish beginning. . . . The*

'*Chronicle*' asked me to resume my articles at five guineas a col. I asked for six."

A most remarkable character, Arnold Bennett. Quite the equal in audacity and success to his own creation, "The Card." He was born a child of the people, the eldest of a family of six, amidst the flame, smoke, mud, and din of the Midland manufacturing district they call "The Potteries"—those grimy, linked up Five Towns which have provided the main reservoir of his literary inspiration.

Beginning with a job in a lawyer's office—he made an excellent lawyer's clerk—he was soon writing in his spare time. Then, by "influence," he obtained a post on a woman's magazine and soon was editor.

Ironically enough, it was a book which Bennett did not believe would bring him in five pounds—and his publishers were inclined to agree—which established him. From it his fortunes, financial and otherwise, began their steep upward rise. This was *The Old Wives' Tale*, which he wrote when he was forty-one.

He had, against the advice of his friends, given up his salaried editorial job and gone to live first in the country and then in Paris. His livelihood depended upon a prolific output of magazine short stories and articles of literary, dramatic, and musical criticisms. He had published a dozen books, none of which had made a great hit. Also he had married a dark, serious, good-looking young Parisienne he had met in the circle of poets, artists, composers, and writers in which he moved.

For years he had wanted to write this story which he called *The Old Wives' Tale*, but it looked a formidable and financially unprofitable task, and at the critical point he had always turned away to lighter and smaller enterprises.

Now, settled at Fontainebleau, he tackled it. It took him eight months. He wrote it with sweat and anguish, and in printed characters. He felt it was good, he knew it was the best thing he had ever done; and he was certain it would never be understood. There he underestimated the artistic penetration and appreciation of his fellow human beings.

The book began to sell slowly, but it went on selling and it is still selling. It made Bennett's name, fame, and fortune. It established him on an unshakable pillar as a serious artist.

Then there was the creator of *Peter Pan*—James Barrie, a young Scot who had come south from the grim, wild barren kingdom north of the Tweed, determined to follow his predecessors and conquer England by peaceful penetration.

Barrie was encouraged to go to London and free-lance by getting several articles taken by a couple of editors who liked his Auld Licht sketches. He lived in a boarding-house in Bloomsbury, amid piles of papers which he went through for ideas for articles, keeping himself so busy that he seldom went out.

Was he happy? Thirty-five years later he told an audience of students that "the greatest glory that has ever come to me was to be swallowed up in London, not knowing a soul. . . .

"Now I am going to tell you about the most romantic fact of my life," he went on. "When my train ran into St. Pancras in the early morning my eye alighted on the most beautiful sight in London. It was the evening bill of the previous night's *St. James's Gazette*, and in large letters on it were the lovely

"'Aye, sir.'

"'Stationed at Barbadoes?'

"'Aye, sir.'

"'You see, gentlemen,' he would explain, 'the man was a respectful man, but did not remove his hat. They do not in the Army, but he would have learned civilian ways had he long been discharged. He has an air of authority and he is obviously Scottish. As to Barbadoes, his complaint is elephantiasis, which is West Indian and not British.' . . ."

And so we must leave the earliest and still the best of English detective thrillers. It only remains to add that he nearly came into the world with a different name. A leaf exists from an early notebook on which the author had written "Sherinford Holmes." One somehow feels that "Sherinford" would never have achieved the world fame of 'Sherlock.'

There must not be forgotten that other writer of thrillers whose real fame was to come after the war—Edgar Wallace. He was partly newspaper-reporter and partly novelist at this time. *The Four Just Men* had received a great vogue from the news that it was the thriller Dr. Crippen had been reading aboard the S.S. *Montrose* when he was escaping from Europe.

Later, Edgar Wallace was to make use of his African experiences in the famous *Sanders of the River* stories which, to many people, still remain the finest things he has written.

Altogether, the "thriller" was entering into its own. Magazine and news-paper editors were just discovering that twentieth-century individual "The Tired Business Man." And for the years to come writers and editors set out to amuse this particular individual.

One great literary career came to an end in 1910. The world learned of Tolstoy's death in November. The chafing of long years against the inconsistencies of the life he had to live as a Russian landowner, with the creed of simplicity he preached so passionately in his books, had torn him at last from his family ties and driven him into the world, alone and penniless. Too weak of body to shake off the family attentions he longed to repudiate, he died in the waiting-room of a railway station not far from his home.

His was a simple, Christian communist creed. He felt it was the gospel which the simple, Christian peasant of Russia needed. He did not realise as he lay dying in that waiting-room that somewhere in London was a bearded Russian, Lenin, devouring the books of Marx in the British Museum reading-room, who would ultimately bring to Russia the creed of Bolshevism and a revolution more complete than that of the French Revolution.

Most of the writers of this time were story-tellers, content to let their imagination roam in romantic cloud worlds. Only at the end of the year did a book appear that, with remorseless logic, shocked a good many people into a realisation of the horror to which the world was swinging rapidly.

The publication of Mr. Norman Angell's *The Great Illusion*, with its thesis that war among great modern communities was financially unthinkable, seemed only another indication of how near everybody was coming to thinking about it.

5

CHAPTER III

GUNMEN IN LONDON

The Sidney Street siege—German Emperor's last visit to London—Pre-war literary favourites—The King's Coronation—Glittering ceremony in Westminster Abbey—Investiture of the Prince of Wales at Carnarvon Castle—Suffragette Movement—Tragedy at the Derby—Big railway strike—The King and Queen visit India—The Delhi Durbar.

I

THE New Year of 1911 was ushered in by a sensational affair in the East End of London. It was to suggest Chicago during the reign of the gangsters after the war.

This was the period when the political exile, the refugee criminal or assassin from the Continent had unrestricted entry into England. The East End of London provided a home for much of the riff-raff of Europe in those days. It was a bunch of characters out of this riff-raff who provided the country with a sensation known as the Siege of Sidney Street.

It is still difficult to believe that the Scots Guards were called out with loaded rifles in the centre of London, that Royal Horse Artillery were rushed to the scene with field-guns, that several hundred armed police were present, and that the Home Secretary, Mr. Winston Churchill, was himself on the spot, all to capture two armed murderers who had taken refuge in No. 100, Sidney Street.

A fortnight earlier a gang of men, interrupted in a burglary in Houndsditch, had fired on the police, killing three of them. Two men believed to be of the gang, whose names, "Fritz" and "Peter the Painter," were now to be on everyone's tongue, had been traced to a house in Sidney Street. The police quietly cleared other people out of the house in the small hours of January 3 and began operations.

At half-past seven, just as dawn was breaking, Inspector Wensley, Inspector Hallam, Sergeant Leeson, and other officers went into the roadway and threw a number of stones at the first floor window. The reply was as sudden as it was dramatic. A perfect fusillade of shots came from the room. Sergeant Leeson staggered back into the arms of Wensley with a bullet in his chest.

"Mr. Wensley, I am dying," he gasped. "They have shot me through the heart. Good-bye. Give my love to the children."

Although severely wounded, so severely that he was afterwards invalided out of the force on a pension, Sergeant Leeson had missed death by a miracle. It was a difficult problem to get him away to hospital, for the whole street was under the range of the murderous Mausers. The doctor who was sent for, in fact, had to climb over a roof and down ladders to get to the wounded man.